The Rel

MW00879179

Communication Cure

Communication Mistakes Almost
Every Couple Makes And How To
Fix Them

By

Joshua Larson

Table of Contents

Introduction

Are you having trouble putting the spark back into your love life? When you come home at the end of the day, are you and your other half content with each other, or do you feel lonely even though you are not alone? You may feel hopeless and lost at this point, unsure of how anything could be the way it used to be again. It does not have to stay that way forever, though.   If you answered yes to either question, the problem is likely that you do not know how to connect with each other. Effective communication is a skill just like riding a bike, and you can learn how in just a few easy steps.

Communicating with your partner in a way you both understand is a science. That is why renowned psychologists and sociologists have studied relationships and the essence of what makes a couple bond for decades. Results from countless experiments have given us the scientifically proven tools we need to repair whatever aspect of our relationships are broken. The advice of these brilliant scientists and testimonies from people in successful relationships laid out here will give you guidance and a hope of making things work with your honey.

As a person in a relationship of many years, I can tell you that heeding the wisdom of others who have gained wisdom from their own experiences is only beneficial. That is why I am here; I have the proper experience to pass down to you what makes love last. Within a few short chapters, you will learn how to improve communication in your

relationship, the importance of listening to each other, and how to weather difficult times and topics together.

I know you are still probably nervous and skeptical. After all, how can a book fix something so complicated and delicate? Well, it can do the same thing that relationship therapy can! You will hear sound advice from many couples' therapists without having to book expensive sessions and miss work. Why are you still waiting around? Every second you spend procrastinating is a second closer to losing your beloved forever. I would never want that for you, and I know you don't want it, either. If you are reading this, you obviously want to repair what is broken. Now you can!

Don't just take it from me; years of comprehensive observation and the practice of scientific formulas will do most of the talking! Learning your partner's "love language" through this popular theory will bring you closer together than ever! I guarantee it.

The Importance of Communication

Since the beginning of time, humans have worked better as a team by communicating with one another. We are meant to be pack animals; we survive better together and thrive on socialization. The lack of positive interaction with other humans can actually negatively impact a person's physical and psychological health.

The relaying of information by socializing with other humans is a large portion of how we understand our world. You cannot learn without a teacher, someone who has lived through an experience you may be going through right now who can guide you out of the stormy sea of uncertainty. We all teach each other specific things, whether they be factual, philosophical, or emotional. Romantic interests do all three.

Over your concurrent lifetimes, you grow together by sharing your experiences and beliefs. Who you choose to spend your life with is important. That person shapes the way you view the world. If you spend your life with a negative, callous person, you become jaded and even depressed. Bright, positive people make the world seem like a wonderful place full of opportunity. How do you want to live out your days: happy and encouraged or sad and pessimistic? The way you act both verbally and nonverbally rubs off on your partner. You are communicating how they should also behave, even if you fail to realize it. Be mindful of that.

Face-to-face interactions establish emotional bonds. We can communicate effectively through the Internet, but without being near each other, you and your partner cannot bond deeply enough to completely trust each other. The worst decision of all on both ends is to date and express your feelings exclusively online. Have you ever heard of the show "Catfished?" For all you know, they could be some perv pretending to be someone else. If you truly want to make a relationship last, you must be physically linked fairly often.

The Effects of Loneliness

Being lonely warps the mind and does physical harm to the body.[1] A neurological study conducted on the brain's response to rejection and isolation found that the emotional pain experienced by the outsider resulted in negative physical symptoms through the anterior cingulate cortex of the brain. Loneliness results in higher stress and a lowered immune system. You can actually get sick from being a loner!

Make no mistake -- experiencing loneliness doesn't mean literally being alone. Married couples can feel loneliness despite sharing a house together. According to John Cacioppo, a neuroscientist and psychologist at the University of Chicago, something as simple as being busy with work keeps you from connecting with your partner and creates a feeling of isolation.[2] The same can happen if you and your mister or missus feel bored in the relationship. When nothing provides exciting stimuli, you turn to yourself and your own thoughts for entertainment. Instead, you will find yourself going over your flaws because you are faced with that ugly internal mirror that we call self-doubt. Humans have trouble dealing with that so much that we create a phantom presence to cope. Believe it or not, that is how a belief in the supernatural flourishes.[3] This is largely due to the lack of the secondary information and solidity that comes with a pack of people of whom you may rely on to confirm or deny your own experiences. Every unfamiliar sound we process becomes uncertain and leaves open the possibility of phantasms, the logic being that we didn't create the noise, so who did? That is why it's supremely beneficial to regularly spend time with your partner. You will legitimately go crazy if you don't!

The Life Saving Benefits of Communication

The reason that partner-to-partner communication is so vital is that this person gives you another perspective and a way of impartially viewing a situation. You are more likely to make rash decisions when no one is around to help process the more rational solutions with you. Your boss could make you so mad that you decide to turn in your letter of resignation the next day with no backup plan. A partner can remind you that keeping your job means keeping a house and food, that you are still advancing your career even if your boss is a jerk. Later on, you will thank the heavens above that they came to your rescue.

Your special someone teaches you wisdom throughout your life. That being said, not communicating with your partner before making big decisions will lead to your ruin. What if you came home one day and said, "Honey, I quit my job." Would your partner's reaction be positive? I sincerely doubt so. The burden of stress falls on them to keep providing while you search for another. You fight more and may ultimately split. I assume you're reading this to stay together, so here's what you should do to avoid heartbreak.

Make time to sit down together and rationally discuss big changes. Come to a compromise and work toward your common interests. You will not only save your relationship, but you'll strengthen the ties that bind you.

The Physical Over the Digital

Being face-to-face at least 80% of the time will further unite the two of you. Texts can't hug or kiss, no matter how many times you write "xoxo" at the end of your message. Fights can start easily just because something you said was taken the wrong way over SMS. Since your partner can't hear the tone of your voice, they have to assume the way you felt. Just the tiniest bit of insecurity will lead to an automatic conclusion that you were being negative.

Relationships thrive on physical touch and intimacy. Remember before, when I mentioned the negative side-effects that come from loneliness? Not being touched for long periods of time contribute to that.[4] Here are a few tips to get that romantic spark and increase in positive communication back in your love life:

Aside from the obvious sexual nature of physical affection, there are little things you can do to keep loneliness at bay and fall in love again.

1. Offer to give your partner a massage after a long and stressful day. They'll appreciate the effort you've shown to help them relax.

2. Lightly caress a shoulder as you pass by to let your lover know that you're thinking of them, even when you aren't sitting down and experiencing something together.

3. Hug them regularly. Hugs provide a sense of security and warmth. Ultimately, it creates a deep bond of trust.

Always keep in mind that consent is key. If your partner does not respond to your touch or tenses up, stop doing whatever you were before. The same applies when they say no or seem to make excuses to get away. Don't break their trust and sense of security by forcing them into uncomfortable situations.

Characteristics of Healthy Relationship Communication

The first way to gauge where you are at in your relationship when it comes to communication is to read over what a healthy relationship consists of. Mark down anything you may be missing, and pay attention when these things come up in later chapters.

The most important thing is that you know each other intimately. It doesn't have to be physical, but you should know things about them that make up their personality. What is his favorite band? What are the names of her best friends? What is their most embarrassing moment? Knowing each other on such a personal level develops a closeness, a deep bond that comes from really understanding them. Do not misunderstand, though. Intimacy has many forms. Most romantic relationships need some sort of physical intimacy to maintain feelings of togetherness. Hugging, hand holding, kissing, and doing things sexually if you are both ready are all parts of a close partnership. Without it, you are left feeling lonely and unwanted.

It is vital that you trust each other enough to be vulnerable and open. If there is any sense of distrust between you, there is no way to be close. Over time, you will drift apart and seek other people that you find you can be completely honest with. That is when a relationship fails. There are simple ways to gauge how much you truly trust each other through evaluating past behaviors and completing trust exercises. (No, I am not talking about the "trust fall." Don't even try it.)

The behaviors that either or both of you have exhibited could be silently communicating to the other that you don't have any faith in them. Are you doing these things?

1. You demand passwords for social media or a phone so you can access your partner's private conversations at any time.

2. You are reluctant to approve of your partner making plans that do not involve you.

3. You interrogate your partner before they leave with questions like, "Where are you going? Who are you going with? How long will you be gone?" Sometimes these questions are welcomed in the context of wanting to make sure that the other person is safe. However, if your tone conveys suspicion, the welcome questions will become very annoying indeed.

4. You read your partner's journal to make sure they aren't saying anything bad about you.

5. When your significant other is gone for longer than expected, you jump to the assumption that they are cheating on you.

These behaviors and habits are not healthy by any definition. If you find yourself doing these things, stop. Try to fix your trust issues in other ways with some simple exercises.

1. Tell your partner a deep, dark secret. No matter how much you love them or how long you have been with them, chances are that there is something you've withheld. Let it go; get it off of your chest. If you bare the darkest parts of yourself to them, they are more likely to trust you.

2. Tell your partner that you love them every single day. It does not matter what mood you're in, even if you're angry, tired, cranky, or upset. It doesn't matter. Let them know that your love for them will never change, no matter the circumstances.

3. Make eye contact for three straight minutes. Yes, this one seems awkward, but the eyes of a person betray real emotion far beyond what facial expressions can. You are getting to

know each other more by studying what their eyes are saying to you.

4. Ask for forgiveness every time you do something to hurt them. You may think you were in the right, but the truth is that hurting your partner with the intent to preserve pride or protect yourself from feeling sad is never okay. Take back what you said or did before it is too late.

5. Show gratitude for what your beloved has done for you. They will trust that you really appreciate them when you point out exactly what it is you appreciate them for.

You two should be able to handle conflict without insulting each other or having the last word. Close partners know when it is time to make a compromise; above all, they strive to work as a team. No one is perfect, but the difference between healthy and unhealthy relationships is that healthy partnerships are based on acknowledging wrongs and trying to make each other happy.

The only good partnership is one where two people see each other as equals. You do equal work in your relationship, and you respect the other person as much as you respect yourself. When one person considers themselves superior, the other tends to be quite angry. You have to admit that it is only rational and fair to expect to be on equal footing.

All of these traits are not just temporary; healthy couples never stop trying to improve. Two people who love each other don't tire of learning about their partner, and each tries to keep the other safe, happy, and content. They rely on communication because it is the only way to maintain a united and peaceful home.

These are expectations you may have for your relationship, and they may not be being met at the moment. That's frustrating, but it is not permanent by any means. You may find that your partner's are also not being met. The solution is first to figure out what the basic expectations are, learn about them together, and discuss what needs to change.

Expectations in Relationships

What People Look for in Relationships

Do you know what a symbiotic relationship is? It is a long-term partnership between two living things in which one or both partners expect to reap benefits as a result. There are three types: mutualism, commensalism, and parasitism. If the relationship is mutual, both parties benefit. If it is commensal, only one being benefits and the other gets nothing. The worst one is parasitism, a relationship in which one being thrives and the other suffers. Romantic relationships can be very similar to all three types. What we all aim for is mutualism, but that means knowing exactly what you both want in order to make your lives the best they can be. If you don't know, you may end up being a parasite. You probably don't want that, do you? I hope not. You can start out by learning what people commonly look for in a partner.

The expectations we have for our partners affects the ways in which we communicate with them. Clearly lay out what you expect from each other in the beginning. If you are having trouble understanding what I mean, here are some examples of questions you should ask so that you can get a better picture of what your partner expects you to bring to the relationship:

- Should the bill be split at dinner?
- What do you like to do most after a hard day at work?
- How long should we be in a relationship before taking things to the next level? (i.e. physical intimacy, living together, etc.)
- Do you want children in the future?
- Which religion do you practice, if any?

Without asking simple questions like this, you both could find yourselves in a sticky situation later. If one person expects the other to eventually want children and the other partner doesn't communicate that they don't ever want kids, how do you solve that later when you're married? Some are trivial and can be worked out with a good conversation, but some of these are deal-breakers. Therefore, it is best to know little facts about what they want before getting serious.

If you two are already shacked up or wed, learn what they expect from you at home.

There are eight main expectations that come from being romantically linked with another person, and these can make or break a bond. You both have a right to these feelings and longings, so figure out if you both are on the same page. If not, either compromise or jump ship before life passes you by without you giving yourself the chance to really experience the fulfillment that comes with a loving partnership.

Kindness and Loyalty

You probably expected me to start off by saying "money," didn't you? While it is true that people may start off listing superficial qualities like money, physical attractiveness, etc., kindness and loyalty give us more satisfaction in the long-term. Your looks fade as you age, and money comes and goes. What does not change is the way we treat other people. Make sure to be nice to the new, bumbling waiter at the restaurant you took your partner to for a date. It's a big indicator of how you will treat them later on when you are frustrated!

Emotional Stability

This one is a no-brainer. We all want someone who is level-headed, someone who isn't prone to violent outbursts or mood swings. Sometimes, people have mental conditions that make being emotionally stable more difficult; while that is understandable, the expectations stay the same. If you are someone dealing with Bipolar Disorder or Borderline

Personality Disorder, you may need to seek professional help before entering the dating scene.

Reliability

In your time of need, who do you expect to be there for you? Your partner, right? That is how it should be, if your relationship is in a healthy place. If you can't rely on your partner to show up when you need them most, when can you? That uncertainty is unhealthy.

Respect

Every person has a right to be respected, and your partner naturally expects it from you. Ridicules and insults show a lack of consideration for their feelings, leaving out an important piece of the puzzle that makes you fit so well. At a certain point, your disrespectful attitude can become abusive. Don't be someone's lesson in what not to look for in a lover.

Interest

The reason you likely got together in the first place was that you both took a greater interest in each other than you did to those around you. As time goes on, you may find yourself listening to them tell the same story for the third time that week. It can be frustrating because you always want to learn something new, and this is not it. You feel like you put one song on repeat for days; I understand because I've been there.

Regardless, you should at least try to seem interested in them. Why are they repeating the story to you? Were you listening closely enough the last time, showing your partner that you care about what goes on in his/her life? Or were you distracted, texting other people or playing a game while they tried to share an important detail with you? Instead of immediately saying, "I know, you have said that already," listen to the story again and see if you missed anything the first time. This may be your partner's way of communicating that you are not meeting their expectations.

Generosity

Do you go out of your way to do something nice for your partner once in a while, or are you so wrapped up in what you want that you let their desires fall to the wayside? Partners should be giving and selfless on both ends. If you never try to prove your love, do you think that person will feel valued? Hint: if you do, you are so, so wrong! This is one of the biggest reasons that romance dies. A lack of effort makes one seem lazy and bored with his or her current relationship. No one wants to feel like a forgotten toy left up in the attic of your mind. Do something more than just saying, "I love you," once or twice per day.

Intimacy

Intimacy does not always entail sexual encounters. It is the ability to be truly vulnerable with each other both emotionally and physically. Let them feel as if they can cast the mask they wear around strangers aside and just be free. (Yeah, that includes the gross stuff like burping and breaking wind in front of each other. Trust me, it gets funnier the more you do it.)

When it does come to sexual intimacy, though, really pay attention to what your partner wants from the experience. Don't leave them feeling unsatisfied or use them to selfishly gain your own satisfaction without caring for their desires. I have personally seen marriages end in divorce based on just this. In the same vein, your partner expects that you respect their sexual boundaries. Intimacy is built on trust; if you violate that trust, you may never be with them on that level again. In fact, you should be going to prison soon after.

Time

There is not a single person on Earth who can genuinely say that they don't need to spend any time with their partner to be happy and satisfied in the relationship. What is the point of being together at all if it serves no purpose and is of no benefit to either of you? Your partner is going to expect you to spend time with them. It may not be possible to spend all your time together if you are both busy or in a long distance relationship, but at least make an effort to put those things aside and spend some time connecting. Video chat if you have to. Just talk to them; do more than shoot a quick text their way. If you refuse to do that simple little thing, you will find that eventually, you don't know anything about the person you are with. Strangers don't build homes together; they build barriers to keep themselves away from each other.

Compassion

Your partner should be able to come to you about something that is troubling them, something they feel they cannot tell anyone else. You should genuinely care about their feelings and be a shoulder to cry on in times of need. If you can't speak freely and have emotional moments in front of your significant other, who can you do that with? Open your heart and show some real empathy. It makes a world of difference when it comes to trust.

Affection

In many TV programs we all grew up with, we see when one part of a couple comes home from work and crosses the threshold, he or she is kissed and hugged by their counterpart. This is what everyday affection looks like to most people. What do you do when you see your spouse or partner after a long day? Ask yourself that, and then consider whether you really make it clear that you like them. A nod, a nonchalant wave, and a grunt in their general direction do not count, and it surely doesn't convey to the person you love that you are truly happy to see them. Notice the way that your partner responds to simple affectionate gestures and continue doing what they seem to enjoy.

Consideration

By now, you should be seeing that the general theme of this lesson is that you cannot be selfish in any way if you expect the flames of love to keep from dying into only embers. This is why you absolutely must put yourself in their shoes. The "Golden Rule" that kids learn in school is, "Do to others what you would have them do to you." If your partner takes issue with something you did, ask yourself if you would be okay if they did it to you. Don't lie to yourself for the sake of keeping your pride. Really picture the situation in your head as if it had gone the other way. I guarantee you will start to understand why you came across as rude or inconsiderate.

Do You Expect Too Much from your Partner?

On the flipside, one or both of you may be expecting too much from the other. You subconsciously measure up your partner at all times, seeing whether they are really good enough for you. This concept is called "relationship entitlement." There is a way to measure how entitled you may be feeling and whether or not it's detrimental to your relationship. This test created by Sivan George-Levi and colleagues[5] is divided into four parts, and you rank each statement from one to five, one being that the statement is not true at all, and five being that you feel it is totally true. Take the test and find out!

Part One

1. I often wonder if my partner is good enough for me.

2. Sometimes I feel that they are not good enough for me.

3. I am obsessed with my significant other's faults.

4. When I am frustrated, I consider ending the relationship.

5. When I'm frustrated, I also consider seeking out a new relationship.

6. When they hurt me, I immediately distrust them.

7. I feel like I deserve more from my relationship that what I am getting.

8. My relationship sometimes fills me with rage.

Part Two

1. I have high expectations when it comes to my partner.

2. I expect my partner to understand me without having to explain my feelings.

3. I can't give up my expectations.

4. I expect my partner to pay attention to me.

Part Three

1. I feel like I am not good enough for my partner.

2. I often wonder if I deserve my significant other.

3. My partner deserves to get more from the relationship than they are currently getting

Part Four

1. I insist on getting what I feel I deserve out of my relationship.

2. I deserve a sensitive partner.

3. My partner is lucky to be with me.

4. If I feel I am not getting what I deserve, I will not accept it.

If you scored high on the first part, you may be entitled and maybe even narcissistic. You pick apart your partner, scrutinizing every mistake and shortcoming and never look at your own. You need to realize that what you are doing is destructive and get help. Understand that no one can possibly be flawless all the time. If you expect perfection, you will be sorely disappointed every day. We are all humans, and we all deserve some lenience.

If you scored high during the second section, you expect sensitivity, understanding, and all around better behavior from your partner toward you. You do deserve a partner who pays attention, but this is a delicate balance; one person can only handle so much before becoming exhausted. You must explain why you feel the way you do when your partner does not seem to immediately get it. Unless by some miracle they happen to be telepathic, expecting them to always read between the lines is unrealistic. Just because you are good at reading people does not mean that your partner will be.

The third section of the test indicates that you may feel you can not tell your partner what you need or want from them, and their expectations aren't being met by you. In this case, your partner may be the one expecting too much from you. Don't be afraid to tell them when you are at your limit. Do everything you can and give an honest effort to be a good partner, but try not to wear yourself out trying to please them. You are just as important.

Part four determines that you can be assertive and expect to be treated well by a significant other. You may notice that the statements are similar to those in the first part, but these are healthier demands of meeting expectations. You deserve the best and happiest relationship possible; it isn't too much to ask for. Just be patient, and never be too pushy. If you want better results, you have to wait for them.

Have your partner take this test at some point as well, and see where your differences lie. Once you know what you do want from each other, try and figure out how you can do those things in your everyday lives.

Now that we have gone over the basic aspects of a relationship that most partners come to expect, let's move forward and learn where you may be coming up short. There is a time-tested scientific formula to solve your problem, and it's all about learning your partner's "love language."

Now that we have gone over the basic aspects of a relationship that most partners come to expect, let's move forward and learn where you

may be coming up short. There is a time-tested scientific formula to solve your problem, and it's all about learning your partner's "love language."

Fundamental Needs in Relationships

Maslow's hierarchy details the basic needs all humans share, one of the most vital being love and belonging. Feeling loved and appreciated are some of the core needs of every human, though everyone has different preferred methods of achieving that security and happiness. The theory of relational maintenance[6] states that there are a number of behaviors that make up the meat of a relationship in order to keep things running smoothly. Dr. Gary Chapman has outlined five of these behaviors through what he calls a partner's "love language."

Through thorough communication, you come to learn the love language of your partner; all five behaviors may not add up to their satisfaction. The combination of a few based on their needs is what does the trick. Finding the correct formula of behaviors leads to a sense of certainty, variety, significance, a stronger connection, personal growth, and the feeling of contributing to something bigger than oneself in your lover. What are the five behaviors that contribute to relational maintenance? Let's find out.

Gift Giving

Sometimes, the giving of material items makes a partner feel that they are of great significance in your life. That means doing more than just the obligatory present for major holidays and special occasions. Bring home a bouquet of flowers because it's a Tuesday, and you love this person so much that you went out of your way on the drive home to stop by the florist just because they like carnations. Stop at the store and buy their favorite candy when they feel blue. Gift giving does not have to be extravagant; tailor what you give to the little things that your significant other seems to find comfort in. An element of sincerity and thoughtfulness is added when your special someone isn't expecting a gift. This fills two different of the eight expectations in one: generosity and consideration.

Quality Time

As our society at large becomes more technologically driven, spending actual quality time with our partners decreases. You can be in the same room, but if you are both engrossed in a game on your phone, you aren't actually spending time together. In 2017 alone, the average Internet user spent almost 6 hours on a smartphone or computer daily.[7] That amounts to roughly 41 hours per week that you could be spending putting your phones down to speak to one another.

Everyone needs alone time, but too much of it can make one feel isolated. Starting out by cutting even two hours off of your screen time will drastically improve your relationship. The more you speak to each other and truly listen with no distractions, the more you will know how to build upon your

41

relationship through learning about each other. Then you won't go crazy or see ghosts or anything like that! Let that be an added bonus. Spending quality time together covers the "time" portion of relationship expectations, as you may have guessed.

If you are stumped thinking about what you should do together, ask your partner! Maybe you could talk over drinks at the cozy coffee lounge down the street or take a walk. Just try to avoid screens as much as possible. Watching movies and TV together can be fun and stimulating, but true quality time involves face-to-face interactions with nothing stopping you from giving your full attention to the person you are with.

Physical Touch

This seems like a silly thing to say. "Duh, everyone needs to be touched!" you may be thinking. Physical affection is indeed key to healthy relationships, but it's crucial to know why. According to a study conducted[8] by three experts in relationships at Brigham Young University, "tactile physical affection is highly correlated with the overall relationship and partner satisfaction. Conflict resolution is easier with more physical affection including hugging, cuddling/holding, and kissing on the lips." So why is touch important? It creates feelings of satisfaction and trust, and it connects the two of you deeply. This satisfies your partner's expectation of affection and intimacy.

Words of Affirmation

Words of affirmation are simply positive and encouraging verbal interactions. They can either be spoken or written in love letters. The crazy thing about doing something so small over time is that it's actually beneficial to your brain and cognitive function. The frontal lobes strengthen, and as they develop, you are more likely to take positive actions in the future without knowing it. Just by saying,

"Great job on your essay, honey! You're going to ace it for sure," both of you are strengthening each other's brains. Besides, it is only considerate to do so.

Acts of Service

If you know that your spouse or date-mate wants you to do something, but they're too nervous to say so, just do it. Do the dishes if they don't feel well that day. Rub their shoulders after work. These spontaneous actions give your relationship the variety it needs to keep things from getting too monotonous. As an added bonus, you will likely experience mutual happiness, yours springing from making them feel content. This is what fulfills the expectation of generosity!

Meeting Needs From Far Away

In long distance relationships, fulfilling these expectations and needs your partner has is challenging and sometimes frustrating. It is not impossible, though. What can you do when you have so many limitations? I'll tell you.

You can always give your partner gifts; it will just cost extra shipping. The upside to such a sad situation is that they'll never see it coming! Because you will probably be ordering a gift online, you have a lot more to choose from than what the local mall can offer. You can customize anything to their liking, too! That makes what you have done extra special.

Quality time is a lot harder to manage when you have a time difference of six hours and plane tickets cost an arm and a leg. I know I said earlier that staring at a screen is counterproductive, but you can use technology to your advantage when you are apart! Any video chatting app like Skype or FaceTime can make for a wonderful date if you try. This is better than a simple call because you get to see your love bug's face!

Physical touch is out of the question, I know. Make up for this lack of intimacy by sending your special someone a more personal gift. Spray a shirt with your perfume or cologne and ship it over. That familiar smell is comforting when they feel lonely or sad.

Make time to talk to each other as often as possible, even over texts or email. Keep up with their everyday life; let them know that you're interested in every detail of their day. This will strengthen your emotional bond and it opens up that doorway to trust and reliability. Now they know they can count on you to be a rock in times where their lives get tumultuous.

Now that you have successfully pinned down how to show love and affection to your partner properly, let's fix the way you communicate with them verbally and nonverbally and how that may be affecting their view of you.

Nonverbal Communication

One of the most important factors of conversation to convey openness and encourage honest communication with your partner is the way you use your body language. The way that you utilize your words and inflect the correct tone is crucial as well, but they are not the only things that you need to watch out for. The wrong stance or gesture can send a different message and produce a different outcome than you were hoping for. There are three main facets of body language that determine how another person interprets a message: posture, eye contact, and facial expression.

Posturing your body in certain ways helps set the tone for what you are trying to say to your partner.[9] Your body's stance based on mood is subconscious, so you may not even realize what you're conveying to the other person while you're speaking. You can override your subconscious neural pathways by carefully paying attention to how you hold yourself. Over time, being more open and relaxed will become second nature. Do daily exercises that focus on releasing tension in the muscles.

Eye contact is proven to be effective for social interactions, depending on the duration of your gaze.[10] We will go over what the proper length of direct eye contact means for your implied intentions in the following paragraphs.

Studies gathered from presidential debates have observed that facial expression is key to likeability. Over the decades, scientists have discovered what makes a successful presidential candidate desirable. The results show that those candidates who were graceful and poised while listening to an opponent's argument instead of making rude facial gestures were favored as likable and more likely to win the race in the long run.[11] The same can be applied when communicating with your partner.

Let's go over the specifics what makes up your body language and talk about the ways you can seem more open and inviting.

What Your Posture Says about You

The way that you hold yourself is the main indicator of your mood. Sometimes, what it silently conveys to your partner is not ideal for opening an honest line of dialogue.

For instance, crossing your arms or holding your shoulders and neck stiffly communicates that you are angry, anxious, and closed off. This is the biggest issue when it comes to keeping the conversation flowing. To seem more interested and attentive, you should relax your shoulders, bring your arms to your sides, and keep your head facing in the general direction of the person speaking. Try to avoid slouching, though; that indicates fatigue or disinterest.

Unless your goal is to seem more confident, do not puff out your chest. Oftentimes, doing so is perceived as cockiness or an attempt at intimidation. It is imperative that you keep from doing this during an argument with your spouse or girlfriend/boyfriend. It only makes things worse, seeming like you are proud of picking a fight. This goes for the way you interact with your date mate's friends of the opposite sex. It is natural to be protective, but scaring off people because of your own insecurity isn't doing you any favors. Learn to stop seeing other people as a threat. Stop making your significant other feel like an object. You are not a dog, and they are not a tree or fire hydrant. Down, boy.

Knowing When and How Long to Make Eye Contact

Staring directly into another person's eyes can reassure them that you are listening and interested in what they have to say. However, there is a delicate balance you must follow to avoid seeming shifty or downright creepy.

Constantly moving your eyes around the room or averting your partner's gaze can make you seem guilty of doing something wrong, which leads to distrust. Trust is essential in an intimate relationship; without it, love and admiration die.

Staring too long makes you look like a creep. The reason that prolonged eye contact creates an uneasy feeling in others is that they feel intimidated and scrutinized. However, couples in love prefer more eye contact than strangers. When you are gazing into your lover's eyes, they may be become physically aroused. Check for the dilation of their pupils for context. If they are enjoying your appraising stare, the pupils will enlarge.[12]

Really, the duration of eye contact depends on the context of the situation. During the middle on a tense or upsetting moment, I wouldn't recommend looking into their eyes for more than a few seconds. A nice, romantic smoldering look can spice your love life up, though.

The most widely preferred method of eye communication is to switch intermittently between looking at someone's eyes and lips. This lets your partner know that you are listening and interested in them. It also comes in handy in a loud room; you can read their lips more easily if you think to look toward them often.

Facial Expressions Between Lovers

Most intimate partners create an unspoken language between each other the longer they are together. An exchange of a knowing look, a raised eyebrow at your wife's crazy aunt that sends you both into a fit of giggles establishes a bond. As for myself, we may discreetly side-eye each other to signal when it's time to leave a boring party. Being on the same page and knowing your partner's feelings before they express them verbally is a surefire way to strengthen your bond.

Now you are prepared to communicate effectively without saying a word, as long as you practice your exercises daily and learn from your mistakes. It is time to take the next step and use what you've learned to navigate difficult times without tearing each other apart.

Verbal Communication

You must also watch out for certain verbal cues; the way that others react to your message depends on which words you use, your tone inflection, and those words that you choose to emphasize.

Choosing Appropriate Words

You may think that your diction does not affect the way that people receive your intentions. After all, no one has time to write a formal letter and rehearse before speaking to others. I get that it may seem trivial, but the tiny details add up over time.

Different words have different intensities and connotations attached to them. When you are annoyed, you are less than angry. When you're depressed, you are more than just sad. Imagine this scenario: your partner comes home from work and leaves their shoes in the hallway, the place you have specifically asked them not to. You get annoyed, and you want to confront them about it. Do you say that you feel miffed, pissed, or furious? No! You make the situation way worse when you bring out the big guns over a trivial thing. See what I mean? What you say determines the outcome of the conversation.

Tone Inflections and Why They Matter

Have you ever had someone tell you that it isn't what you say, but how you say it that matters most? What they are talking about is the tone of your voice and how it affects your message. If you are excited that your spouse got a promotion at work, put some emotion behind your congratulations! Chances are that you read the last sentence in your head a certain way. The exclamation point at the end had a sort of sound to it. That is the way you should speak when you are excited or happy.

Likewise, apply the same sound you hear internally with a period at the end of a sentence when you are trying to convey solemnity or firmness.

There is one way of speaking that doesn't have its own punctuation mark: sarcasm. That is what you get when you use an inappropriate tone on purpose. If you're visibly unhappy but you say, "Oh, that's just great!" in mock happiness, you are applying a tone of sarcasm. Avoid doing this at all costs if you want a positive outcome, especially with your partner. Doing this is often inflammatory and will lead to an argument. The only exception to this rule is if you are both feeling the same way about a situation and mocking your collective misery will bring a laugh out of them. Otherwise, just say no.

Emphasizing Words Works

The main parts of your sentences that you use to communicate your intention to another should be subtly stressed. In this example, your significant other just lost an important family member. Read the following two sentences in your head and think about which one seems more appropriate:

"I'm so sorry for your loss. Is there anything I can do for you?"

OR

"I'm *so sorry* for your loss. Is there *anything* I can do for you?

The first option seems monotone, kind of like you are just consoling this person out of obligation. The second stresses that you feel sympathetic and that you truly do want to help them feel better. When you emphasize the word "anything," it suggests that you mean you would do whatever it takes to ease their burden. Just be sure to not overdo it. Too much emphasis seems insincere and sarcastic, something we discussed earlier.

Now you are prepared to communicate effectively, as long as you practice your exercises daily and learn from your mistakes. It is time to take the next step and use what you've learned to navigate difficult times without tearing each other apart.

How to Manage Conflicts

The most complicated and confusing thing to successfully manage in a relationship is a conflict. Tensions run high, and in the moment, you both say things you shouldn't to try and "win" the argument. You end up regretting it later, but some things cannot be taken back. It is a challenge for all couples, even those who have been together for decades. It's never too late to change your bad habits using the skills we've already talked about and the advice here. Shall we continue? I think so if you want to keep your love alive.

Setting the Right Environment

There must be some level of security and trust in your relationship before you can even begin to talk about the rough stuff with your partner. If you have hidden important information from them in the past or have been cruel during previous arguments, you have to put in some effort to regain that level ground you two were on in the beginning. The most important ways to create a calm and safe space are fairly simple. You just have to know where to start and what to do.

Trust

The foundation of any relationship is built on mutual trust. Imagine that you plan to go on a cruise. You wonder which company will give you the experience, and the facts are laid out before you. One cruise line has had a multitude of issues on several excursions: the power goes out, the sewage tank backs up, and people have gotten food poisoning from the buffet. The other is one you have booked a cruise with before, and you had no major problems on your trip. Which are you more likely to choose? The same principle applies to your love life. If you do not give your partner the environment that they need, you are going to find yourself alone. So how do you gain this person's trust again?

Building Trust Over Time

The best time to begin gaining the trust of another person, especially a romantic interest, is right away. No relationship is going to last long if, after a month, you still haven't done anything to deserve unwavering belief. How do you go about building it, though? It's elementary!

Never assume that anyone is going to trust you without a bit of work on your part. Earn it; stick to what you say you will do and do it! If you consistently prove that your promises are sincere, you'll gain the trust of your partner.

Be supportive; encourage your sweetheart when they do something they are proud of! When you refuse to share in their enthusiasm, you build a wall. They likely won't come to you with good news anymore because you do not seem to care.

Forgive your partner when they make a mistake. No one is going to be perfect. Some things aren't worth forgiving (abuse of any kind, chronic unfaithfulness, etc.) of course, but most things are worth getting past and moving on. Each mistake is a lesson for both of you. If you want to make it work, you will.

Never fight in public or make a scene online when your partner screws up. Disagree and air your grievances in private. For one, no one wants to be unwillingly dragged into your drama, and most importantly, making a big deal in front of prying eyes is embarrassing for the both of you and will ultimately solve nothing.

What to Do if You've Broken Your Partner's Trust Before

What creates an unstable environment and causes your partner to feel betrayed? According to David Bedrick J.D., Dipl. PW, counselor and former teacher at the University of Phoenix, these are the two factors that make for a betrayal: breaking a promise or agreement whether spoken or unspoken, and that person being hurt as a result.[13] Maybe you were unfaithful, or you hid a life-changing secret from your partner. Whatever you did, you betrayed that person and hurt them emotionally and mentally. That is what creates an environment of distrust.

After you lie to someone, you may find yourself wondering what compelled you to do such a thing. This can be scientifically explained, though it isn't an excuse to continue on with bad behavior.

Stephen Stosny, Ph.D., relationship counselor and author, asserts that the biggest reason people betray their partners is to feel an adrenaline rush.[14] Adrenaline is released in the brain during times of stress, causing a "high" feeling similar to that of cocaine. Lying generally causes stress to a person because they have something to lose if caught. Consider whether feeling high is more important to you than your relationship. Get a grip, and start fixing your issues.

The first step to regaining trust is to acknowledge both to yourself and verbally to your partner that you did something wrong. Apologize in a sincere way. Your apology is not coming from the right place if you shrug the blame onto them for your actions. Half-apologies like, "Sorry you feel the way you do," or "Sorry, I didn't mean to/I didn't know" are unacceptable. It is not about making excuses for yourself. It's about what you did to your partner. The way you word it is important; make amends by validating the other person's feelings.

You may want to assure them that you will never betray their trust again; don't. If they already doubt you, they are not going to believe in your promises. Let your actions speak for you in the future. Be better by avoiding the situations and people that encourage or tempt you to lie to your partner.

Anyone who wants to get in the way of what you have is *not* a real friend.

Be patient and give your relationship time to grow. You won't get results overnight, but you will get them sooner if you start now and keep building that trust and faithfulness consistently.

Respect

If your boss came in today and told you, "I think you are a piece of garbage and bad at your job, but I'm not going to fire you," would you be pissed off? Of course, you would! You would feel disrespected and want to quit then and there, right? That is how relationships are. If you insult or mock your partner, they will get sick of it and decide to break up with you. You absolutely cannot treat anyone like trash and expect them to put up with it indefinitely.

The Two Types of Respect

Marriage counselor Daniel Dashnaw[15] breaks down the two different types of respect that a relationship needs to last, those being "appraisal respect" and "recognition respect." Let's go over each more in-depth.

Recognition respect refers to the way that humans, in general, should acknowledge that every individual has a right to free will and self-agency. Oppressing your partner, keeping them from speaking their own thoughts or preventing them from doing what they want to do is a breach of respect and is emotionally abusive. If you expect your partner to submit to you, you lack recognition respect for them.

Appraisal respect is the "give and take" of any relationship. It relies on your ability to compromise, your patience, and your willingness to listen to your partner's needs and wants.

You can't just pick one and stick to that. A healthy relationship needs both aspects to thrive. Otherwise, it's just an abusive, toxic mess that hurts everyone involved.

Staying Respectful During Arguments

If you feel guilty thinking back over all the times you have treated your lover badly during heated arguments, try to get to the root of *why* you did it.

Were you feeling insecure about yourself at the time? Insecurity in ourselves and the frustration that comes with it causes us to lash out at our partners. The insults we throw at the people we love are often a mirror of what we are feeling about ourselves.[16]

Did the other person say something negative toward you first? The human ego kicks into overdrive when that happens, so we do anything we can to defend ourselves and preserve a sense of pride.

Both of those questions are root causes of the disrespect you may show to your partner, and they happen subconsciously. You are acting on instinct. The best thing to do when you realize why you're being so bitter is to call for a time-out and calm yourself down. The simplest way to be more respectful is to think logically about your situation instead of letting your emotions lead you around.

Four Ways to Maintain Respect in a Relationship

There are four parts to putting your respect into action and maintaining that peace and harmony in your relationship: mutuality, reciprocity, accommodation, and acceptance (refer to above citation for source).

Mutuality is the concept of setting up boundaries in your relationship and agreeing to abide by them. *Reciprocity* ensures that you both promise to keep your judgments and assessments of one another fair and balanced. You *accommodate* one another by respecting the others' limitations, even if the formerly agreed upon boundaries change as you grow and change as individuals. *Accept* that you are both different, and you will, therefore, have different beliefs and dreams.

Remembering and observing these four concepts every day will foster a peaceful and happy partnership.

Approaching Difficult Topics

By now, you have successfully created an atmosphere of trust in your home where you both can be vulnerable with each other. From now on, talking things out will be easier. However, every relationship goes through troubles at one point or another, and it's crucial to address the problem and solve it together. Sometimes, the topic is incredibly personal and touchy, and you may have a tough time trying to navigate. Have no fear! There are five very common topics and events in relationships that cause conflict. Do any of these resonate with you?

Common Causes of Conflict

There are quite a few stressors in our everyday lives that can trigger an argument with the ones we love most. What are those stressors, and how should we resolve the issues that arise with our partners? Let's find out.

1. Financial trouble is one of the most common triggers for a fight in a relationship. There are different scenarios as to how it gets started. The two of you do not agree on how and when to spend your money, you can't decide who pays for what on a date, or one of you has recently lost a job and the other person feels distressed about being the sole breadwinner. It is understandable that this can cause a ton of stress, but fighting about it does not provide a solution. You need to sit down and plan

ahead of time how to spend your finances, who pitches in for a certain bill or date, and a contingency plan for being fired. When you know ahead of time what you can do in a period of confusion or tough situations, the weight will surely be lifted off of your shoulders.

2. Something I have seen couples struggle with quite a bit is how to split up responsibilities when it comes to chores, kids, and errands. If only one person works, they often feel entitled to doing less at home because they may feel their partner did not work as hard. That makes the stay-at-home partner insecure and hurt, leading ultimately to a fight. If you are the one working and feel this way about your partner, remember that you live there, too. Those are your kids, too. It takes two people working as a team to make a happy home. Sizing each other up and holding things over one another is unhealthy. Again, plan ahead of time. Make

a chore chart and stick to it. Have the kids pitch in if they are old enough! More helping hands make for light work.

3. Moving causes an immense amount of stress in couples. Both parties must agree on a place to live, whether moving is best for each person's work life, and when the moving should be done. Then there is the sweaty, hard work that comes with packing and unpacking. The whole ordeal is exhausting, and tensions rise when people are tired. In this case, plan far ahead. You can't always know when you might have to move, of course, but talk about what both of you want from each area far before you ever think of moving for real. That way, when the time comes, you will already have a good idea of what to look for. If you need to, write everything down and review it when the time comes.

4. A lack of intimacy, sexually or otherwise, is frustrating. If you are a person who is interested in sex or want to be affectionate and your partner isn't as forthcoming with it, you feel put out and unattractive. The best thing to do for this sort of problem is be honest with your partner about your feelings. How are they supposed to know they are not meeting your needs if you never tell them?

5. Politics and religion. These are firmly-held core beliefs that indicate the views that a person considers to be of utmost value. Ideally, you two would have discussed these topics before you decided to be exclusive or get married. If you never got around to it and those things are coming up now, settle your differences by talking to each other about *why* these beliefs are so important to you and what they mean about how you want to live your lives. Do not try to convert each other; that is the biggest no-no of all. When you preach to

your partner and try to get them to act like you, you are telling them that their beliefs are less important than your own. If you want any sort of peace, you must have a mutual understanding and agree to let your significant other be who they want to be. If the way they act due to their political or religious standings is unbearable, use this book to help you with your new partner when the time comes.

If those brought up memories of arguments you have had in the past, reflect on how they ended and if the problem is truly resolved. If not, have no fear! There are tools you can utilize to keep the conversation as smooth as possible, as given by Susan Krauss Whitbourne, Ph.D.[17]

1. Only put it off for so long. When you have something this important to discuss, you will need time to cool off and prepare rational talking points; that is completely

understandable. Just remember not to avoid it for too long; letting the emotions fester and exploding later is unhealthy and detrimental to your relationship. Also, tell your partner that you would like to discuss an issue ahead of time so they can prepare as well. Saying something like, "We need to talk," without at least telling them what about causes a lot of unnecessary anxiety on their part.

2. Stop adding caveats to the ends of your sentences. Give the bad news first, and the good after. As an example: "Our car needs to be fixed and it's going to be expensive, BUT I saved up some money in our account so we won't be struggling." If worded the other way around, the recipient does not know what to expect and it triggers anxious feelings.

3. Stay optimistic and reach a compromise. Both of you may have a different end-goal to the

conversation in your mind, and you'll be severely disappointed when you do not end up getting what you want. If you have to compromise, I promise it will not be the end of the world. Your relationship is by no means doomed just because your beloved would like to go out with her friends more often and leave you at home to your own devices. Instead of pouting about it, reach a mutual decision to set how many days per week you are comfortable with her doing so, and give in a little to meet her needs for other social interaction; negotiate.

Communicating Through Intense Emotion

Getting to the Root of Your Feelings

There are quite a few reasons why you may be upset or arguing with your partner. You can't solve your problem if you do not even know what it is. Here are some common feelings and issues that can spark these arguments or overwhelming emotions:

1. **Jealousy**. While feeling jealous of your partner sometimes is natural, too much of it can lead to being possessive or territorial. Eventually, you can drive your partner away if you do not sit down and recognize why you feel so jealous. Dr. Susan Krauss Whitbourne[16] takes us through the process of easing feelings of envy and jealousy by taking us through these questions and tips. Are you uncomfortable because your love has too many friends of the opposite sex? Get in touch with your emotions. Why does that make you feel possessive? Once you really reflect on the root cause of your emotions, make a strategy for redirecting your thought patterns. This is when you talk to your partner about the way you feel and why. Maybe they can soothe your fears.

2. **Insecurity.** Feeling down about your self-image reflects how you behave and how you speak to your partner. You tend to become more pessimistic and look for reasons that your partner may not love you anymore when that simply is not the case. If you find yourself thinking things like, "I'm not good enough," dissipate those ugly lines of thinking with logical reasoning. Remind yourself of all the good times you and your spouse or boyfriend/girlfriend have had. Listen to the compliments they pay you and reflect on those instead of moping.

3. **Feeling unsatisfied.** Maybe your relationship has been stuck in a rut lately. Things aren't exactly great in the bedroom, and you two have hit a routine that feels monotonous. Feeling unsatisfied with your love life can be frustrating, and you come to resent your partner. This is when you sit down with the other person and ask what you both could do

to spice things up. Never accuse them of being boring; this rut was caused by both of you for lack of spontaneity. So what can you do to pick up the pace? Go on dates regularly, learn a new hobby together, and try new things in the bedroom if it's what you both need. You will find that your frustration dissipates as long as you keep working at it.

4. **Your feelings may be unrelated entirely** to goings on in your relationship. Stress that comes from work or anger from tensions with a friend can bleed into your romantic life. Your built up emotions spill out because you want to vent, but it comes out the wrong way. Maybe something your partner said triggered a nerve because it was similar to the way your boss criticized you earlier. When that happens, your beloved disappears and the source of your anger appears instead. We use the people we love as punching bags because we know they will still love us regardless of

what we say. That isn't right; take a breather and ask to blow off steam by talking to them and if you already took out your feelings on an undeserving person, apologize and explain why what they said poked at a sensitive place inside.

Exercising Self Contol

If you have any hope of keeping your emotions in check over the course of the argument or discussion, you absolutely must have a solid measure of self control. This may mean learning to hold your tongue when all you really want to do is scream at your significant other and take out all of your negative feelings on them. If you are still reading, you know by now that doing this is what probably got you here in the first place. I know that resisting the temptation to just go berserk is hard, sometimes *really* hard. So what should you do when that urge arises?

1.) Reward yourself for good behavior. Whenever you fight the irrational anger and win, treat yourself to a snack. The next time the tense situation arises, your brain will subconsciously really want that snack later, so it will encourage you not to let your ego out of its cage. Progressively make your rewards for yourself bigger until your desire to fly off the handle is diminished completely.

2.) Monitor yourself and notice behavioral patterns. What is it, exactly, that sets you off in emotionally charged discussions? Is there a phrase, facial expression, or tone that your partner uses that just really enrages or upsets you? If you notice it, talk to them about it or avoid bringing up anything of that topic unless it is important enough to warrant a serious talk.

3.) Set goals for yourself. Something like, "I will not raise my voice with my significant other this week," is a good place to start, and you can build up over time. When you fail, do not punish yourself too hard, but definitely refrain from doing anything your brain could mistake as a reward. We all mess up, but we shouldn't let ourselves get my with our mistakes too often or they will become regular behavioral patterns again.

These are small ways to help yourself that drastically change the future of your willpower. Now you can focus on coping with your stress and know that you can stick to the strategies without throwing caution to the wind.

Coping Mechanisms During Times of Stress

We have all been there – we struggle to remain calm when a certain argument or discussion has us all choked up. Fighting tears or anger while speaking to a partner is difficult, I know. There is a simple scientific explanation for the awful way you feel when your emotions get intense, and you can override those feelings with a few coping mechanisms.

When you get upset or anxious, your sympathetic nervous system starts working overtime. Your heart rate shoots up, your temperature rises, a heavy feeling settles in your chest, and you feel like your throat is closing up. These symptoms are all because of our "fight or flight" response. But why does it flare up in situations where we are not in actual danger?

According to researchers studying at the Harvard Medical School[17], any stressful situation is perceived as a danger to our brains. The amygdala, the part of the brain responsible for emotional processes, sends a signal to your hypothalamus. The hypothalamus then releases chemicals like adrenaline throughout the body, creating this storm of symptoms.

Instead of running or fighting with your partner, though, use some coping tips to take a pause, calm down, and reenter the conversation with a clear and rational mind.

Pace your breathing! Doing breathing exercises will counteract the symptoms of your "fight or flight" response[18]. Breathe in through your nose for about four seconds, hold it for two, and release through the mouth for five seconds. Hold your breath again for a couple of seconds and repeat about six times. The purpose of this exercise is to slow your heart rate, making your entire body relax.

Lower your expectations. You may be a perfectionist, and you want everything to come out exactly the way you pictured it. The truth is that no situation will turn out exactly according to plan. Your partner will not often react the way you want them to, so try not to overthink and over plan what you are going to say or do.

Before the discussion even happens, you can maintain your cool with five simple steps, according to Dr. Susan Krauss Whitbourne[19]:

1. Avoid the situations which will cause an emotional flare-up. If you know that your partner will be angry if you bring up a serious topic in the car, wait until you get home to talk about it.

2. Only talk about what you know you can handle. If something is still too overwhelming

and will spin your emotions out of control, give yourself more time to think about it.

3. Shift your focus on the most important points; bickering about the small details that really aren't worth your time and energy distract from what takes priority, and you become less likely to actually get through the conversation.

4. Change the way you think about a problem. Instead of dwelling on the negative, think about all the ways your life could go right if you move past your difficult emotions. Changing your thoughts and reinforcing them with positive thoughts and hope will motivate you to take the steps you need with your partner to overcome the snag in your relationship.

5. Control your responses. If your partner says something that makes you angry or sad, put

those breathing exercises into effect and refrain from flinging out a nasty retort.

Responding to an Angry Partner

When your significant other seems to be constantly angry with you, you begin to think that maybe the problem isn't mutual, but lies solely with them. That can be discouraging, but there are ways to respond that can diffuse the tension and help this partner feel better.

1. **Encourage them to let their feelings out.** Ruminating on what makes them angry and bottling it all up will make things much worse when their emotional responses are triggered. Over time, this pent-up rage becomes integrated with this person's personality and it becomes much harder to get rid of those feelings in a healthy manner. Scientists at Japan's Kansai University[20] conducted a study on how suppressing anger relates to a

person's core personality traits. As expected, those who suppressed anger often became more temperamental over time. Curbing this unhealthy decline is part of your job as a partner. If your honey feels that they can come to you to vent safely, you both avoid painful arguments later.

2. **Understand that their anger is not always personal.** Your partner could just be having a rough day; that does not mean that they get to walk all over you, but ask your other half what happened and help them calm down with the breathing exercises you learned. You do not have to be dragged down to their level over something that has nothing to do with you; practice being more patient with them.

3. **Speak in neutral tones.** Tone inflections can drastically influence any interaction. Think back to times when the way someone spoke

to you sounded condescending or hateful; it may not have been what they said, but rather, how they said it. You will notice that in your partner sometimes and want to respond in the same way to hurt them back; refrain from doing so. Control your tone, and they will eventually realize that they may be speaking too harshly.

4. **Interactions don't always have to end in an argument.** Angry people pick fights over nothing; it is not your job to react. Let it go without making snarky comments. That person will likely feel foolish afterwards and want to apologize for their own bad behavior. See how much easier that could be resolved than if you gave in to your pain and replied?

5. **Help your partner with mastering their anger issues.** A healthier outlet would be for them to join some type of gym where they can

hit, kick, or punch something. Boxing lessons would be fun for the both of you! Of course, find a way to word your proposition gently; saying, "I think you should go to the gym," will not work, as I am fairly sure you already know.

Avoiding Destructive Conflict Resolution

You have just had an argument with a significant other and though the discussion is over, you don't seem to feel any better. Why is that? Not all conflicts are solved positively; you two may have been practicing negative strategies for resolving conflicts. You end the argument, but the issues between you still remain. These are the things you should do during a heated moment to end on a positive note[21]:

1. **Stop searching for an attack.** When you do not take the time to read between the lines, you hear only accusations and go into

defense mode instead of really paying attention to what your partner needs you to hear. If they say, for instance, "You really hurt me today when you did this thing," and you only hear the "You hurt me," you are less likely to go into the rest of the sentence with an open mind. Look for the root cause of their feelings instead of focusing on your own.

2. **Use "I" statements.** The best way for you to avoid making your message look like an accusation is to refrain from starting any sentence with "you." Instead of saying, "You made me feel this way," say something like, "I felt really upset when this thing happened." These small changes in your verbal communication will keep your partner from being defensive.

3. **Find the good in your partner.** Picking this person apart over their faults is incredibly

harmful to their self-esteem and your argument. Compliment something they do and address the current problem at the same time. Example: "Honey, I know you are gentle and kind, but I feel like what was said earlier was a little harsh. Can we talk about it?"

4. **Ask yourself why your argument is happening;** what is your real problem? Which needs are not properly being met, and are they fixable or something you have to just get past? You may be expecting far too much from your partner, and that is on you, not them. We'll talk more about that in just a minute.

5. **Accept that you are different people,** and you can't really agree with each other on everything. Listen to their side, and speak on your own. Agree to disagree sometimes.

6. **Do not interrupt.** The fastest way to frustrate your significant other is to speak over them at every turn, offering unsolicited advice and demanding that they listen to you because you feel that the solutions you provide are the best path to take.

7. **Stop trying to have the last word.** Why do you feel that you must "one-up" your partner? If you have nothing relevant or important to add any more, it is far better to close your mouth and go calm down. Otherwise, you look childish and foolish.

Just being mindful of these small conflict resolution strategies will make all the difference in your relationship. Over time, arguments will be few and far between. Instead, you will be able to sit down and have adult discussions without descending into madness. What if you haven't even gotten that far?

What do you do if you and your partner do not converse at all?

Handling a Complete Lack of Communication

"But Joshua," you say, "you have given everyone tips on how to improve upon their communication methods, but what about me? My partner and I don't communicate *at all*." Oh dear, are you in a predicament. A total lack of communication in a relationship is a sure sign that soon, everything will end -- that is, if you continue down that path. It does not have to be that way; you just have to make the first move.

Odds are that you started out close and drifted apart over time, and you barely speak now. Something must have gone wrong along the way. There are five fatal mistakes[21] when it comes to communication in relationships, and they can be devastating if done over and over again.

The Five Biggest Mistakes in Communication

1. **Avoiding your problems.** You were too afraid of starting an argument, so you just never aired your grievances with each other. That leads to some serious repression, and you find outlets in unhealthy ways. You turn to angrily posting on social media about your partner, you gossip about them to your friends, and you may even turn to another person intimately. Trust me, your partner knows that you are up to something. You need to say something before it all blows up in your face.

2. **Never bothering to ask personal questions** makes your significant other feel as if you do not care about them. Humans always change; we never stop evolving emotionally. You may feel as if you know everything there is to know about them, but that simply isn't true.

3. **Not making time to verbalize how much you appreciate your partner** comes off as selfish, especially if you expect them to do it for you. Fawn over your sweetie pie sometimes, and you will notice the bond between you growing closer.

4. **A lack of empathy for the troubles your partner may be going through** will leave them isolated. They will not come to you, because you don't seem to understand or care to try.

5. **Being passive aggressive** is just about the worst thing you can do. When you were in elementary school, giving your friend the silent treatment over an argument was the norm. You are an adult now; you cannot just thumb your nose at someone, especially not the person you love just because you are grouchy. You will eventually shut down all

communication through just being petty; no one wants to deal with a grouch all the time.

Reflect on whether or not you may have done these things before. Are any of these a recurring pattern? If so, this may be precisely why you and your lover are giving each other the cold shoulder.

Ways to Improve Your Interactions

Just because your relationship is currently broken does not mean it can't be fixed. Even if you've made all five mistakes countless times, there is still hope. If your partner has stuck around for this long, it means that he or she is still clinging onto the idea that you can be whole again. Good news for them -- you can! But where do you begin? Right here, of course! Use these easy strategies everyday, and you two will be a dynamic duo in no time.

1. **Approach the conversation promising to withhold all judgement.** We criticize our significant others far too harshly sometimes. We are all guilty of it; you are not alone, trust me. Just because we all do it from time to time, though, does not make it right or fair. No matter what your partner may be telling you, wait until they finish their piece and be open minded. For instance, your husband comes home and says to you, "Oh gosh, honey, I really messed up. I crashed the car into a pole today; I'm so sorry." If you react with judgement and tell them that they obviously weren't paying enough attention or that they mess up too often, do you think they will ever want to come to you again with something like that? Will they be open to being vulnerable with you? No, probably not. Instead, talk to them about what needs to be done to fix the car; reassure them that mistakes happen and promise that the two of you will figure it out

together. Never reaffirm the insecurities they have. It is just plain rude.

2. **Request things of your lover, but do not demand that they do what you say.** What is it that our parents told us growing up? Ask nicely. Be polite. That applies far past the age where you want to go over to Jimmy's house for a sleepover. It's a life lesson. Ask your partner to take the kids to school or do the dishes. Don't just demand that they do it. You are being inconsiderate and quite possibly abusive, depending on what it is you are trying to force the other person to do. If they say no and you have the ability to do it yourself, just do it! It is so easy to just get up and do something if someone else is busy or exhausted. If you both are, leave it for a day if it can be left. Something small is not worth fighting over. Just make plans in the future and lay out who does what. Compromise.

3. **Be supportive and enthusiastic.** Share their joy, sorrow, and contentment. When things are going well for your other half, cheer them on! Validate their feelings. When they fall on hard times, offer a shoulder to cry on. Let that person know that no matter what happens, no matter how many ups and downs there are to life, they can count on you. Just be there!

4. **Prove your commitment to your significant other every day.** You don't have to rent a gondola and serenade them on it or anything; just do small things to show them that you care. Leave them little love notes to find around the house. Make it a point to say, "I love you," even if you are angry or upset with them. Tell them to be safe when they leave the house. You never know when the last words you say to them really will be the last ever. Make them count. Over time, your sweetie pie will be more relaxed and will

return the favor for you. When you reach out and show that you care, so will they.

5. **Think of the positive, and do not dwell on the negative.** When your partner fails to text you back, do you assume the worst? "Oh no, they must be in an accident!" or, "She is probably out cheating on me right now." Chances are that their phone is just off or dead. Calm down! Blowing up their phone is annoying; just say no to that.

6. **Trust your partner, and make sure they know you do.** Why are you with someone if you cannot trust them, right? If you do, show it. Unless that person has slighted you previously and you both are working on it, you have no reason to be suspicious of their actions. Avoid creeping through their personal messages or reading their journal. When you constantly try to catch them in the act of doing

something they shouldn't, you convey to them that to you, they aren't a good person. Over time, they will get tired of feeling scrutinized and either do the same to you or leave.

7. **Stop thinking in absolutes.** Black and white reasoning is highly destructive. "If you don't want to be intimate tonight, it means that you think I am unattractive." In print, it seems ridiculous, doesn't it? That is because it is. It's an absurd way of thinking, yet so many fall victim to it. Your partner just isn't in the mood, more than likely. It isn't on you; they just feel like doing something else, and that is perfectly okay. Not everything has to be one extreme or the other.

8. **When you mess up and they ask you to apologize, do not make the apology an opportunity to gain sympathy.** Fess up, validate their emotions, and fix the problem.

Saying things like, "I know, I'm a terrible person and I hate myself," shifts the focus on your emotions, not theirs. That is selfish and manipulative. It isn't a real apology, and you know it. If you feel insecure, address that later and seek comfort from them when the time is right.

9. **Be vulnerable.** Letting people in your head completely can be terrifying. Someone has probably used your vulnerability against you at some point in time. That was wrong; I can see why you may not be so forthcoming again, but this is a key aspect to your relationship. Communicate your feelings. You are not weak, you are not pathetic for coming to your partner with your deepest thoughts and emotions. Like I said, you have to trust them.

10. **Listen.** When your partner knows that you aren't attentive, they start to believe that you

do   not love or care about them at all. It isn't the truth, but your actions speak louder than your words. What other way is there to interpret it? You must actually pay attention to their words and feelings in order for them to trust you enough to speak to you more.

We should go over listening in depth, since that is the hardest thing for people to truly understand. When you think you're doing a good job, you may be messing it up big time; I don't want that for you, so I am going to make you understand what it takes if it's the last thing I do.

The Importance of Listening to your Partner

Being truly attentive when your partner speaks will make them feel important, loved, and satisfied. Listening effectively can prevent conflicts before they happen, and when they do happen, opening your ears and eyes to the message they are relaying to you will end them quickly.

"But I am listening!" you protest. Not likely, pal. We all would like to think we pay close enough attention to our significant others, but almost none of us do. Why not? We just get lost and have no idea what to improve upon. Luckily for all of us, the tools and strategies we need to help us out are easy enough.

Are You Really Listening?

Even when there is no conflict to get through, you need to recognize the bad habits you may have and stop yourself from doing them. Things you may not have even thought were destructive can be grave mistakes, indeed. I have five questions for you when it comes to whether you really listen or not:

1. While your partner is speaking, are you already thinking of what to say next?

2. Are you only listening to them to pacify their needs, only doing so because you really have an ulterior motive or goal?

3. Are you being critical of them and the way they speak, listening just to judge them?

4. Do you zone out periodically because you started daydreaming?

5. Do you often interrupt the middle of their sentences?

If you answered yes to any of these, I am sorry to tell you that you haven't been doing your part in the relationship. You are not listening as well as you should be. I know what you're thinking: "Well, wise guy, what am I supposed to do about it?" You learn! Learn and practice. Hold your horses, because I am about to give you everything you need to know.

Active Listening

Yes, there is a distinction between regular old listening and active listening. The difference is that in one scenario, you may not be giving your partner your full attention or you don't react to the things they say in an appropriate way. Being active involves showing genuine interest in a person's message for you. You do not interrupt, you sit and zone in without daydreaming about what you might eat for dinner. It can be

difficult at first if you have problems with your attention span. There are medical reasons you may be having trouble. Let's talk about that.

The Underlying Issues of a Short Attention Span

There is a stigma around the mental condition called ADD, or Attention Deficit Disorder. It may call to mind an image of a little kid doodling on the desk during a lesson. "That is a made up disease pushed by doctors so they can medicate children!" you cry. You say that, but you can't seem to focus on another person when they speak. You get bored easily, and some days, your head feels fuzzy. I'm no doctor, but you may need to see one. Of course, you can't just use it as an excuse any time you want to justify being lazy in your relationship. However, it is a real condition and you need help.

The same can be said for partners on the autism spectrum. Autism is almost always portrayed as a severely disabled person who can't complete daily tasks without help, someone who talks differently and is prone to emotional fits. There is nothing wrong with those people, but it is called a spectrum for a reason. You may function just fine on your own, but you face issues when it comes to socializing or making eye contact. It makes you nervous. Again, seek medical advice if you feel your symptoms match.

Would you rather be diagnosed with an illness and face a stigma or lose the person you love? You decide, but I think you know what the better option is.

Now that you've read this lovely little P.S.A., let's break down the parts of a conversation and how those parts tie in with the way we listen to and receive messages.

The Four-Ear Model

The University of Munich's Michaela Pfundmair and colleagues[22] came up with a four-part model that breaks down the modes of communication that we use in our everyday lives and how they relay messages to other people.

The first factor that determines how we give and receive messages we put out is the factual information in what we are saying. If we know that what someone says is true, we are inclined to believe and listen more closely.

The second factor is self-revelation. The information about yourself that you want to share with someone should be interesting or relevant to the conversation to keep the other person or people attentive.

The third deals with your personal connection to your conversational partner. Appeal to your bond when speaking to someone based on what you want to say.

The final part of the four-ear model is how you appeal to another person. What is your goal, your proposition to them?

When dealing with an intimate partner like a boyfriend, girlfriend, spouse, etc., if you two are having a conflict, you want to listen closely to what emotions they are appealing to and how they are relevant to you. Obviously, the most important focus is not factual information when you're going at it over who loves who more. You'll focus more on your relationship.

Believe it or not, the way we communicate and get others to listen is based on the levels of oxytocin being released in their brains. If you are trying to ask someone for a favor, they are more likely to listen to what you're saying and consider helping when their levels of oxytocin are higher. Oxytocin has many functions, and one is making someone more empathetic. By making your appeal to them clear and concise, you are likely increasing the production of the chemical.

Listening During Conflict

We, as partners, find it hard to listen to unpleasant conversations or touchy truths we avoid when it comes to our actions. That is counterproductive to what we are trying to accomplish through communication. Small acknowledgments of what your partner is saying can ease tensions. Here's how:

1. Put away all distractions. Leave your phones in another room, and turn off your ringer. When an alarm grabs your attention, you stop listening to your love. Turn off the TV, mute and put on hold anything that keeps your full attention elsewhere.

2. Ask questions. If you find something hard to understand or get confused, ask a relevant question. Scenario: your spouse has just said, "The way we are doing things isn't working anymore.

3. Something needs to change!" To show that you are listening and serious about making your relationship work, ask something like, "Do you have any ideas for what we can do to fix things?" Remember, use a neutral tone when you say this. If you use an exasperated tone, it implies that you doubt their capability of doing their part to give suggestions.

4. Recognize your own faults. If you find yourself pulling away from an open and honest dialogue and causing more problems, stop and give the other person a turn to speak. Apologize for being disrespectful, and move on.

5. Make eye contact. The most annoying thing to me is noticing that the person I'm speaking to has their eyes on everything else but me. We spoke about this in the "Nonverbal Communication" section of the book. Go back and read it again if you forget why eye contact is important.

6. Respond to a question in a timely manner and react appropriately. A lack of expression and leaving questions unanswered implies that you are not interested in what someone else has to say. You are making things far worse when you give no indication that you are paying attention.

How to Improve Your Listening Skills

You know now how to keep your cool and listen during a tense moment, but you do not really know what to do in a normal conversation. Of course, there are similarities in the way you should behave, but things are just a little different. I want you to be able to distinguish between techniques and apply them appropriately.

1. Maintaining eye contact is appropriate in this situation as well, and you have had an eyefull of my tips on that. Just keep doing what you are doing, and you will be fine.

2. Now relax. In an argument, you may be paying attention, but you stare at your partner just a bit too long or your muscles are tensed. In that scenario, it is to be expected. In a normal discussion, though, you look like a weirdo when you keep your gaze fixed on

your partner like a hawk or have your shoulders all bunched up. If you have problems with anxiety, I understand that this may be hard to do. In that case, breath in deeply through the nose and out through the mouth. Do those breathing exercises we talked about until you are sure you can remain chilled out!

3. Don't judge your partner before you know the whole context of the story. Even if the end makes you feel no better, remember that you

   are here to rely on each other, not to tear each other down. Keep your mind open at all times, no matter what is being said.

4. Never interrupt on purpose. We all have days where we accidentally speak over each other a few times; that is completely understandable. What you do not want to do,

though, is purposefully try to get your thoughts out before the other person finishes their own sentence. In fact, don't try to finish their sentences for them. I know you are really excited to share your own perspective, but rushing other people like that is rude.

5. Occasionally give feedback to your significant other when the conversation calls for it. If you are asked a question, answer it honestly and politely. Try not to ask questions until they are done speaking, though. Again, that is just another way to interrupt.

6. Search for what your partner wants you to read with their own nonverbal cues. You know what to look for now, so that should be easy! You will find it less difficult over time to decipher their body language and read the lines.

Applying Your Listening Skills

Great! Now you know how to really receive everything your partner is saying with no distractions or confusion. It is not always enough, though, just to listen. You need to prove that you have actually been doing so through your actions. How? It's really easy, I assure you. Try doing some of these things just to let your lover know that you heard them loud and clear:

1. Bring up something that your significant other said to you in days before and ask more questions about it. It is always nice to know that someone is interested in what we have to say. Something as small as that will earn your major brownie points.

2. Whether your partner has said so verbally or nonverbally, improve in an area that you know you need to work on. Pick up on your

partner's tone when they talk about chores and errands that need to be done. Are you helping enough?

3. Take a mental note of all the times your special person has reacted positively to something you said or did. Keep doing those things as long as you are comfortable with them. Listening to and noticing the subtler things will make them feel like you read their mind. Nonverbal positive reactions can present themselves in facial expressions, relaxed muscles, and affectionate reciprocation through kisses or a gentle touch.

4. You should also watch for whatever your partner reacted negatively to and try to avoid doing it again. They may be afraid to tell you that they don't like what you are doing because they feel that it makes you happy. Just ceasing these activities can be a huge

relief. Nonverbal negative reactions can be things like tensing up muscles, not speaking at all when they were previously really chatty, and making excuses to get out of whatever it is.

5. Offer to let them vent to you before they have to ask. Your significant other may have been reluctant to ruin your mood or burden you with more stress. Show them that a partnership means taking on even the bad things together. Offer them a hand when they seem to be struggling.

If you apply your newly learned skills every single day, you will see results; I guarantee it. Really, what's an hour out of your day to show your partner that you're paying attention in the grand scheme of things? We spend more time than that playing games on our phones!

Using What You Have Learned

Your head is probably spinning from trying to remember every single thing you need to work on. If it isn't, kudos! For the rest of you, you will need some sort of daily guide until you get the hang of things. Okay, so let's lay out some of the daily practical applications of how you can improve communication in your relationship!

Speaking the Love Language of your Partner

First, you need to find out what it is (obviously). After you do, how do you put it into effect?

- Do a chore your partner is falling behind in or just do something you know needs doing. Make the bed, take out the trash, take the kids to school, do the grocery shopping, vacuum and dust, or wash the car! There are just a few ideas for you.

- When your significant other comes home, express physical affection toward them. Give them a shoulder or foot massage. Kiss them, hug them, hold their hand. You do not have to go all out with candles, roses, and a dance. (unless you want to -- then go for it!)

- Tell them how grateful you are that they work so hard for both of you every single day. It does not matter whether they have a traditional day job; anything they do, they do for the betterment of your home. Express your gratitude.

Learn Something New

No matter what time of day or night it is, practice your listening skills by asking them about themselves. Learn something about their new hobbies, ask about how work/school went. Really, just make the focus of the conversation about your special person and what their life is like. If you are nearing the holiday season, you can even be sneaky and ask about what they like in a subtle way. You can use their answers to buy an amazing gift that they will never forget! You can never go wrong when you just ask.

Keep Your Cool

Every now and then, you two are going to squabble over something petty. If the situation is more serious, actually refer back to the chapter on conflict. If not, remember your breathing exercises. Keep your tone level, and do the same for the volume of your voice. Yelling helps no one. If you need to very badly, take a break from your argument and spend some time calming down before getting back into things.

Maintain Self Control

If you are feeling any type of negative emotion, remember not to take it out on your partner. Even if the things you are feeling directly relate to them, be kind and understanding. You catch more flies with honey than with vinegar. Get to the root of why you feel the way you do, and consider more constructive ways to work them out instead of releasing your frustrations onto someone else.

It's All About Give and Take

Remind yourself that every healthy, strong relationship requires both people to compromise. The spoiled toddler inside all of us demands that we get our way every time; never listen to it. As adults, we are responsible for reaching some kind of agreement that benefits everyone involved.

Be Trustworthy

Let your actions prove to your significant other that you are the person they can come to for everything. Be faithful to your partner. Throw aside all judgment when they come to you with their vulnerable moments or embarrassing/dark secrets. Show them the equally dark or embarrassing sides of yourself;

let your partner trust that they can really be themselves around you.

R-E-S-P-E-C-T

Like that Aretha Franklin song says, "All I'm asking is for a little respect when you come home." That is all your partner wants -- to feel respected by you! Do that by taking what they say to you seriously. When they feel wronged, acknowledge your own flaws. Try to improve. Share home responsibilities equally to let them know you don't just see them as a maid. You also need to know that there is a fine line between playful teasing and ridicule. Playing around is fine! Insulting someone whether it is because you find it funny or because you really want to hurt them is not okay.

Say Those Three Words

All anyone wants to hear at the end of the day is that the person they love loves them in return. Those words are so easy that a toddler can say them, and it is free! What's holding you back? Say them every morning, after every conversation, and every night before bed. Make them believe it with all of their heart. After all, you never know when the last words you say really will be the last ever. Get over yourself and say, "I love you!"

Communicating with your partner every day really is as simple as that.

Conclusion

Finally, you are sufficiently equipped and ready to get out there and conquer the problems that tear you and your sweetheart apart. There have been a lot of tough lessons to learn on the way, a lot of unpleasant truths that you have had to face about the ways you fall short. That's okay, though! You have come out stronger and better for it, and you get to be your honey's hero. I am also sure it was a relief to realize that some problems just aren't your fault. Use these strategies to step up and be better; be gentle and patient when explaining to your partner where they need improvement as well.

Always be conscious of your words and behavior, remembering that misunderstandings happen. When they do, do not beat yourself up. Apologize, internalize, and grow! You are both only human; forgive each other.

From time to time, re-evaluate yourself to make sure that you are meeting your significant other's needs. Are they meeting yours? If not, sit down and discuss what needs to change. Listen, do not interrupt, and never accuse them of hurting you on purpose.

Through the good and the bad, be there for the person you love most in the world. Prove your feelings for them by speaking their love language. With time, they will come to trust you and rely on your again. Be patient! Nothing shows results overnight. Relationships are like gardens -- tend

to them, pull up the weeds every once in a while, and watch your love flourish into something beautiful!

In summary, remember these things: listen, learn, respect, trust, and let things go. I hope that you take to heart everything you have been taught here. You'd be a fool not to! After all, you are learning the secrets of professionals that normally, you might pay thousands for! You're welcome, by the way.

My last piece of advice would be to have your partner read this as well. That is the real first step toward better communication. Maybe when they're done, you two could spend *quality time* together *talking* about what you have learned. See? I am helping you in more ways than one!

Now you are back on track to happily ever after. I wish you the best; may you both become the wise old people that another struggling couple needs.

References

1.) Eisenberger, N., Lieberman, M. and Williams, K. (2003). *Does Rejection Hurt? A fMRI Study of Social Exclusion*. [online] Science Mag. Available at: http://science.sciencemag.org/content/302/5643/290 [Accessed 16 Nov. 2018].

2.) Cacioppo, J. and Patrick, W. (2009). *Loneliness Can Kill You*. [online] Available at: https://www.forbes.com/forbes/2009/0824/opinions-neuroscience-loneliness-ideas-opinions.html#5888cc337f85 [Accessed 16 Nov. 2018].

3.) Blanke, O., Pozeg, P. and Hara, M. (2014). *Neurological and Robot-Controlled Induction of An Apparition*. [online] Cell.com. Available at: https://www.cell.com/current-biology/fulltext/S0960-9822(14)01212-3 [Accessed 16 Nov. 2018].

4.) Floyd, K. (2013). *What Lack of Affection Can Do to You* [online] Psychology Today. Available at: https://www.psychologytoday.com/us/blo g/affectionado/201308/what-lack-affection-can-do-you [Accessed 16 Nov. 2018].

5.) Whitbourne, S. (2014). 19 Ways to Tell If You Expect Too Much From Your Partner. [online] Psychology Today. Available at: https://www.psychologytoday.com/us/blo g/fulfillment-any-age/201411/19-ways-tell-if-you-expect-too-much-your-partner [Accessed 27 Nov. 2018].

6.) Dindia, K. (2003). Maintaining Relationships Through Communication. [online] Available at: https://books.google.com/books?hl=en&l r=&id=8LCRAgAAQBAJ&oi=fnd&pg=PA 1&dq=relational+maintenance+theory&o ts=wDmarc5HTJ&sig=IgmHDeg4w1qolA

uT0ZUwFaKJQgE#v=onepage&q=relati
onal%20maintenance%20theory&f=false
[Accessed 17 Nov. 2018].

7.) Egbert, N. and Polk, D. (2006).
Speaking the Language of Relational
Maintenance. [online] Research Gate.
Available
at:https://www.researchgate.net/publicati
on/233241159_Speaking_the_Languag
e_of_Relational_Maintenance_A_Validit
y_Test_of_Chapman's_1992_Five_Love
_Languages [Accessed 17 Nov. 2018].

8.) Gulledge, A., Gulledge, M., and
Stahmann, R. (2006). Romantic
Physical Affection Types and
Relationship Satisfaction. [online] Taylor
& Francis Online. Available at:
https://www.tandfonline.com/doi/abs/10.
1080/01926180390201936 [Accessed
17 Nov. 2018].

9.) Mlodinow, L. (2012). How We
Communicate Through Body Language.

[online] Psychology Today. Available at: https://www.psychologytoday.com/us/blog/subliminal/201205/how-we-communicate-through-body-language [Accessed 27 Nov. 2018].

10.)   Schulz, J. (2012). Eye contact: An introduction to its role in communication. [online] MSU Extension. Available at: https://www.canr.msu.edu/news/eye_contact_an_introduction_to_its_role_in_communication [Accessed 27 Nov. 2018].

11.)   Stewart, P. (2012). Connection found between audience reaction, candidate debate success. [online] ScienceDaily. Available at: https://www.sciencedaily.com/releases/2015/07/150727140817.htm [Accessed 27 Nov. 2018].

12.)   Murphy, C. (2011). Learning the Look of Love: In your Eyes, the Light the Heat. [online] Scientific American Blog Network. Available at:

https://blogs.scientificamerican.com/guest-blog/learning-the-look-of-love-in-your-eyes-the-light-the-heat/ [Accessed 27 Nov. 2018].

13.) Bedrick, D. (2013). Building & Repairing Trust: Keys to Sustainable Relationship. [online] Psychology Today. Available at: https://www.psychologytoday.com/us/blog/is-psychology-making-us-sick/201310/building-repairing-trust-keys-sustainable-relationship [Accessed 27 Nov. 2018].

14.) Stosny, S. (2014). The Betrayal Epidemic. [online] Psychology Today. Available at: https://www.psychologytoday.com/us/blog/anger-in-the-age-entitlement/201401/the-betrayal-epidemic [Accessed 27 Nov. 2018].

15.) Dashnaw, D. (2018). Healing Intimate Relationships Worldwide.

[online] Couples Therapy Inc. Available at: https://couplestherapyinc.com/13-ways-to-show-respect-in-marriage/ [Accessed 27 Nov. 2018].

16.) Whitbourne, S. (2013). 6 Ways to Break Free from the Trap of Jealousy. [online] Psychology Today. Available at: https://www.psychologytoday.com/us/blog/fulfillment-any-age/201307/6-ways-break-free-the-trap-jealousy [Accessed 27 Nov. 2018].

17.) Harvard Health. (2011). Understanding the stress response - Harvard Health. [online] Available at: https://www.health.harvard.edu/staying-healthy/understanding-the-stress-response [Accessed 27 Nov. 2018].

18.) Allen, S. (n.d.). How To Keep Calm When You Are Stressed, Angry or Overwhelmed. [online] Dr. Sarah Allen Counseling. Available at:

https://drsarahallen.com/keep-calm/ [Accessed 27 Nov. 2018].

19.) Whitbourne, S. (2015). 5 Ways to Get Your Unwanted Emotions Under Control. [online] Psychology Today. Available at: https://www.psychologytoday.com/us/blo g/fulfillment-any-age/201502/5-ways-get-your-unwanted-emotions-under-control [Accessed 27 Nov. 2018].

20.) Takebe, M., Takahashi, F. and Sato, H. (2015). Mediating Role of Anger Rumination in the Associations between Mindfulness, Anger-In, and Trait Anger. [online] Research Gate. Available at: https://www.researchgate.net/publication /281431642_Mediating_Role_of_Anger_ Rumination_in_the_Associations_betwe en_Mindfulness_Anger-In_and_Trait_Anger [Accessed 27 Nov. 2018].

21.)   Whitbourne, S. (2015). 17 Rules to Guide You Through Any Conflict. [online] Psychology Today. Available at: https://www.psychologytoday.com/us/blog/fulfillment-any-age/201501/17-rules-guide-you-through-any-conflict [Accessed 27 Nov. 2018].

22.)   Guise, S. (n.d.). 5 Communication Mistakes That Kill Relationships. [online] mindbodygreen. Available at: https://www.mindbodygreen.com/0-14106/5-communication-mistakes-that-kill-relationships.html [Accessed 27 Nov. 2018].

Disclaimer

The information contained in **"The Relationship Communication Cure"** and its components, is meant to serve as a comprehensive collection of strategies that the author of this eBook has done research about. Summaries, strategies, tips and tricks are only recommendations by the author, and reading this eBook will not guarantee that one's results will exactly mirror the author's results.

The author of this Ebook has made all reasonable efforts to provide current and accurate information for the readers of this eBook. The author and its associates will not be held liable for any unintentional errors or omissions that may be found.

The material in the Ebook may include information by third parties. Third party materials comprise of opinions expressed by their owners. As such, the

whole or in parts. No parts of this report may be reproduced or retransmitted in any forms whatsoever without the written expressed and signed permission from the author.

Made in the USA
Middletown, DE
19 March 2019